The *D*iscipleship *S*eries

Other titles in the series

15

Ways to a More Effective Prayer Life

Published by CWR, Waverley Abbey House,
Waverley Lane, Farnham, Surrey GU9 8EP, England.

Copyright © 2001 by Selwyn Hughes
First published in Great Britain 1982
ISBN 1 85345 174 6

Typesetting: Start
Printed in Finland by WS Bookwell
Illustrations: Helen Reason
Front cover image: Helen Reason

15

Ways to a
More Effective
Prayer Life

Selwyn Hughes

Contents

Preface

Prior to entering the Christian ministry I heard an elderly preacher say that that everyone has a problem, is a problem or lives with a problem. At first I was a bit sceptical of that statement but no sooner had I entered the ministry than I found those words to be true. Problems of all shapes and sizes were brought to me and, feeling ill-equipped to deal with them (my Bible College training taught me a lot about God but little about people), I went to the United States for training in the area of biblical counselling. How glad I am that I took time out from my work as a pastor to focus on discovering the biblical causes that lie beneath human problems and how to utilise the truths of Scripture in correcting them.

The booklets in the Discipleship Series set out to confront some of the difficulties or issues that Christians come up against when seeking to live as Christ's twenty-first-century disciples. They are written with two groups of people in mind. Firstly, those who are looking for something that will speak clearly and concisely to their present need and secondly, those, such as counsellors or ministers, who want to offer some additional material to people they are seeking to help that will supplement their own individual counselling efforts.

My prayer is that God will make these brief but prayerfully written booklets a blessing to those who seek to become Christ's true and faithful disciples.

Selwyn Hughes

Introduction

"I've been a Christian for a number of years now but I find prayer so utterly boring. I've read a number of books on the subject, but none of them seem to give me a handle on the issue – a workmanlike approach that will bring my prayer life in line with what other Christians appear to enjoy. Can you help me?" The speaker was a middle-aged school teacher by the name of Mark who had come for counselling on the subject of prayer. He said that, after his conversion, he felt instinctively that he ought to pray, but whenever he got down on his knees and tried to talk with God his mind went blank. As a result he was growing increasingly frustrated in relation to the matter of personal prayer.

I explained to Mark, as I do to all who seek my advice on building a more effective prayer life, that our rate of progress in the Christian life is greatly determined by our power *in* prayer. If we don't pray then we don't grow spiritually – it's as simple as that. I then went on to share with Mark a simple strategy for developing a meaningful prayer life, but I stressed that this was to be seen only as a scaffolding and not a structure. "Using these principles", I said, "you can build your own pattern of prayer. The important thing is to develop a system or an approach to prayer that is suited to your temperament and personality. Once you have achieved that then the scaffolding drops away – mission accomplished."

The principles I shared with Mark in helping him to establish an effective prayer pattern have been worked out in hundreds of hours of personal counselling and I have shared them with thousands of Christians in seminars, conferences and other types of meetings. In sharing them once more through these pages I hope they help you as much as they have helped a host of others.

There is no way to get on in the Christian life without the disciplined practice of prayer. The way to grow "in Christ" is to talk with Him: to talk with Him daily and to talk with Him for more than just a few moments. Many Christians find prayer difficult. Some use printed prayers. Others memorise a sequence of words which they use at the beginning and the end of the day. Others, convinced that prayer is only meaningful when it is spontaneous, pray only when they *feel* like praying. But the most important practice of the Christian life cannot be left to the unpredictability of feeling. Every Christian needs to establish for themselves a systematic approach to prayer – one that is simple and uncomplicated yet flexible enough to allow for individual spiritual growth.

1

Breathe
a prayer
for **help** as you begin

When a tiger attacks a victim the first objective is to slit the throat of his victim with his sharp claw. When the victim is no longer able to breathe, he is finished. Satan, the enemy of our souls, seeks above all to cut off our spiritual breathing because he knows that when this is accomplished we die of our own accord. As you seek to develop greater prayer effectiveness be alert to the fact that the devil will do everything in his power to discourage you and divert your attention to other things. He doesn't mind how many committees you sit on, how many sermons you preach, how much evangelistic literature you pass out, how many meetings you attend, providing you spend little or no time in prayer. So, before we go deeper into the subject, send up a little telegrammatic prayer right now, asking God to help you see that you are beginning something which will make all the difference between weakness and strength, between defeat and victory.

You will find that the more you pray the more you grow in spiritual things. Prayer tones up the whole life. You can never be better in life than you are faithful in prayer. If prayer lags, life sags.

If you know how to pray you know how to live, if not then you merely exist. When you pray you are like an electric bulb in the socket, full of life and power. When you don't pray, you are like that bulb out of the socket – lifeless.

A lady once said to me, "You don't say anything very original, but you seem to push God's message right into my heart." I've cherished that as a pure compliment. Actually, a Christian doesn't really originate anything; he transmits. One Old Testament writer said, "There is nothing new under the sun." Every important principle of living has been enunciated before; we simply repeat in new forms what has already been uttered and expressed in days gone by. God is the origin of all we are and all we have; we simply pass on what has been passed on to us. Once we learn the art of receptivity, that is opening ourselves to God in prayer, we have learned one of the greatest lessons of life. Luke tells us that one day Jesus withdrew into the wilderness to pray, and adds "the power of the Lord was present for him to heal" (Luke 5:16–17). These two things follow as cause and effect – prayer and power. They have been described by someone as "the Siamese twins of the spiritual life".

Francis of Assisi had this as his motto: "More than I can." We can do more than we think and accomplish things beyond our abilities when we pray. Many Christians think of themselves as reservoirs with a fixed capacity, but if we are men and women who give ourselves to prayer then we are more than reservoirs – we are rivers. We are attached to infinite resources and therefore we have boundless possibilities.

2

Establish a **definite time**

Some Christians complain that their busy lives leave them no time to pray, but as it has been said, "If you are too busy to pray, then you are busier than God intended you to be." So build a fence around a certain part of the day and reserve it for contact with God through prayer. The best time to pray is in the morning when your mind is fresh and the day is still before you. The psalmist said, "... in the morning I lay my requests before you and wait in expectation" (Psalm 5:3). Don't try to find a time for prayer – *make* time. If you go through the day trying to fit a prayer time into your schedule you will fail. Make it the first priority after you awake from sleep to keep a prayer appointment with the Lord.

We need not, and should not, limit our prayers to such appointed moments with God. We can pray anywhere – in the street, on the way to work, travelling in a bus or train. But these spontaneous and unpremeditated prayers must be seen as *extras*. Growth and development in the Christian life demand firmness with ourselves in relation to fixed and definite times for prayer. One great prayer warrior said, "Those who do not provide for a *quiet time* in the morning, do provide for an un-quiet time during the day. The probabilities are that you will have to take time off during, or at the end of the day, for regret, for penance, for eating humble pie, or for realising a sense of frustration, emptiness and futility." This is not to say, of course, that if for genuine reasons you miss your quiet time in the morning God is going to "punish" you by siphoning off your spiritual peace. He loves you too much for that. No, what it means is that when we deprive ourselves of a regular contact with God through prayer we remove ourselves from the power that makes for effective Christian living.

A diver who would regard it unnecessary to check that his airline is in working order before he descends into the depths, would be no more foolish than the Christian who descends into the stifling atmosphere of today's world without getting his breathing apparatus of prayer connected with the pure air of heaven above. When we become spiritually anaemic and pale, it is usually due to self-inflicted asphyxiation.

A traveller tells of journeying through the Panama Canal. He says, "The great sea gates were closed upon us. We, who had sailed the oceans, were blocked, shut in, helpless, our freedom gone. But lo, we felt a great lifting, great fountains were opened up from beneath, and to our astonishment that great ship was lifted thirty-five feet in just seven minutes. Then the gates opened and we glided out on a higher level, out on the bosom of Lake Gatun." The morning prayer appointment does that – it shuts you in with God, the door closes upon you and you seem so enclosed, so helpless. And then God's infinite resources begin to bubble up from within, you are lifted silently, powerfully, effortlessly, without noise or strain, on to a higher level. The door opens and you glide out on to a higher level of life. Those who practise daily contact with God through prayer are often amazed how easily they transcend worries and fears and resentments, and live on a higher, more positive, level. The answer is quite simple: it's the result of being shut in with God.

William R. Inge reminds us: "It is quite natural and inevitable that if we spend an average sixteen hours of our day in thinking about the affairs of the world, and only five minutes in thinking about God ... this world will seem two hundred times more real to us than God." The great Christian and philosopher, Blaise Pascal, once declared, "Nearly all the ills of life spring from this simple source, that we are not able to sit still in a room." What, if in that stillness we meet with God? Would not all our fears, our hesitancies, our doubts, be hushed in the quiet of God? Isaiah said, "We have been waiting for thee, be our strong arm; morn after morn, deliver us, all forlorn" (Isaiah 33:2, Moffatt). When we "all forlorn" meet with Him "morn after morn" then He becomes "our strong arm", our Deliverer. To those who say they do not need to have specific times of prayer because they pray anywhere and everywhere, I would say you cannot maintain the spirit of prayer unless you take specific times for prayer. Experience has shown that unless one has a regular organised time for prayer then it loses its energy, its force and its power.

3

Keep your **appointment** even when you don't feel like it

I t would be wrong of me to lead you to believe that your prayer times will always be full of vitality and spiritual excitement. At times, prayer can be drudgery. The most noble vocations have their times of drudgery, and prayer has them too. If our prayer times were conducted solely on the basis of feeling, then our moments of communion with God would be few and far between. We must learn to pray and keep our appointment with God whether we feel like it or not. If we have an engagement with a friend, or a business appointment, we keep it, regardless of our feelings – sickness or emergencies apart. We would regard someone as lacking in common courtesy if he or she cancelled an engagement with a friend, just because they "didn't feel like it". Are we to be less courteous with God?

In talking to hundreds of Christians about the subject of prayer, I have found that one of the most common misunderstandings is the view that prayer is only effective when it arises from an eager and excited heart. Nothing could be further from the truth. Many of the great saints of the past who have written on the subject of prayer believed that great waves of feeling belong only to the early stages of discipleship. This does not mean, of course, that the higher you rise in the levels of discipleship the less feeling will be involved. It means rather that the more experienced you become in prayer the less dependent you will be on feeling, and the more dependent you will become on faith. Faith, not feeling, measures the efficacy of prayer.

A number of things happen to us when we pray despite our lack of feeling and inclination. Firstly, *the meek submission of our will deepens our spiritual lives.* One great spiritual leader, Dr E. Stanley Jones, said, "The one business of human living is to keep our wills coinciding with the will of God in self-surrender and constant obedience." The human will is so self-centred, so stubborn, and so recalcitrant, that it wants its own way in everything. When, by an act of will, we decide to spend time with God *even though we don't feel like it* we take the steps to break our will of its inherent self-centredness and thus train it to respond more to God than to our own carnal desires. One man put it to me like this: "The more I make my will respond to God, the easier it becomes to take God's way in *everything.* The will, it seems, gets the message that God is first in my life and it is learning to respond more to God's way than my own way." Once we learn how to make our human wills submit to the divine will we have discovered one of the greatest secrets of the Christian life: one that opens our whole being to God's endless resources of life and power.

Secondly, our resolution to engage in prayer greatly strengthens thought control. Many Christians are discouraged because they are unable to control their thoughts. But one of the main reasons why they are defeated is because they never *practise* thought control. The apostle Paul exhorts us to focus on this matter by "bringing every thought into captivity to the obedience of Christ" (2 Corinthians 10:5, NKJ). The more we practise thought control, focusing the core of our thought life, the imagination, on the things of Christ, the more expert we will become in the matter.

When we confront every negative thought pattern, the thoughts that lead us away from the place of prayer, and stubbornly refuse to let them have their way, we take an important step toward mastery of our thoughts.

Thirdly, committing ourselves to prayer when we don't feel like it develops powerful muscles in our faith. Just as physical exercise builds up muscles in the human body, so does praying against inclination greatly strengthen the tenacity of faith. Jesus placed great emphasis on faith. He never said "Thy feeling hath made thee whole" but "Thy faith hath made thee whole." The old Welsh theologians used to say that "faith develops only as it is exercised". They claimed that everyone has a "measure of faith" (Romans 12:3) but we can only rise higher in the scale of faith as we use the faith we have. The more we use it, they said, the more powerful it becomes.

If a man or woman finds themselves in doubt about their ability to develop, and sustain, a systematic and methodical prayer life, let them undertake a planned programme of prayer for a month. Let them keep a daily appointment with God, even though they may not feel like it. Let them pursue the task with firmness and resolution. I would be greatly surprised if, at the end of the trial period, they did not discover such a joy and rapture that nothing, positively nothing, would in future keep them from the place of prayer. The experiment would end in an experience.

4

Find a **suitable place** in which to pray

If it is possible find a quiet place to which you can withdraw and where you can feel secure from interruption. Jesus said, "When you pray, go away by yourself, all alone, and shut the door behind you and pray to your Father secretly" (Matthew 6:6, Living Bible). There are times, of course, when Christians are to pray together (see Matthew 18:19) but Jesus is talking here about individual prayer, not corporate prayer. And the secret of effective praying as individuals is to pray in secret. All Christians need to have, if possible, a quiet spot in which to pray, for such a spot will gather spiritual associations which will quicken their imagination whenever they go there, and will call them to prayer even when inclination ebbs. Praying with friends, or with your family, is a necessary and vital part of prayer, but to build up your personal relationship with Christ you need to spend time with God *alone*.

I realise, of course, that for some, the finding of a quiet place to pray is almost an impossibility. Those who live in overcrowded homes, or share a room with a non-Christian in a college or university, will find it difficult to find a private spot in which to pray. Difficult, but not always impossible. It's amazing how the

Lord leads His children towards appropriate private spots and places when once He sees within them a desire for intimacy with Himself. A young man I once counselled, a member of a large family, all of whom, apart from himself, were unbelievers, asked me to pray with him that God would enable him to find a quiet spot in which he could conduct his daily devotions. We prayed together, and then some days later he telephoned me to share a most amazing story. He said he was on his way to work that morning and noticed a minister about to park his car in a small car park adjacent to a church. He felt led to go over to the minister and share with him the fact that he was a Christian. During the course of conversation the young man told the minister about his problem of not being able to find anywhere private in which to pray. The minister said, "Well, don't let it be a problem any longer. I come to my church every morning at 7am to do my own praying. I have a spare room which you can use if you wish, and when I am away then you will be able to borrow the key and use it indefinitely."

I have known innumerable instances where Christians, desirous to spend time alone with God and unable to do so because of circumstances, have been directed by divine guidance to private spots or places in the most remarkable manner. And even if a private place for prayer is not available, don't let this keep you from a time of regular communion with God. A friend of mine, a young businessman and the only Christian in a large family, told me how he overcame the problem of not being able to find a private place in which to pray. He travelled on an early commuter train from Guildford, Surrey, to Waterloo, a journey that takes about 45 minutes. "I spend almost all of that time", he said, "in contact with the Lord. Although the train is often crowded I have learned to become deaf to the distractions. As soon as the train pulls out of the station I climb the stairs in my soul to the sacred chamber of my imagination where I picture myself meeting with the Lord Jesus. Every morning He greets me with a smile and says 'I'm glad you've come'." Admittedly it took him some time to learn the secret, but with patience and perseverance you, too, can learn to build a chapel in your soul.

It's astonishing how real a secret chamber can be, built within the heart by imagination and consecrated thought. Dr W. E. Sangster tells, in one of his books, the story of Charles de Foucauld who lived a hermit's life in the deserts of North Africa. He was sometimes invited by the French officers to their Mess. On some occasions the officers told stories that passed the bounds of propriety. Rather than leave the Mess, he said, he learned to sit still and withdraw into the secret chamber of his soul. When he was asked if he felt upset by some of the stories passed around he said he never heard them because he was in his own "oratory". That kind of oratory any man or woman can, with determination, build within his or her own soul.

It should not be forgotten, also, by those whose prayer life is hindered because of lack of privacy, that it is always possible to go for a walk with Jesus. Christmas Evans, one of the greatest preachers Wales has ever known, tells of walking along the base of Mount Snowdon one evening and entering into such a spiritual tête-à-tête with the Lord that it transformed his whole being. How true it is, as the hymnist put it:

Where e'er we seek Thee thou art found
And every place is hallowed ground.

5

Go into your prayer time
relaxed and **receptive**

You will not go far in prayer if you approach it with a tense spirit as though you were going to force God to give you what you ask. The spirit of prayer should be what someone described as "alert passivity". Alert passivity means that while your spiritual, mental and physical sensibilities are awake and alert to God yet they are relaxed and receptive.

In order to put yourself in an attitude of alert passivity you must first begin with the body, the outer framework of prayer. If you don't get much physical exercise then follow these few simple guidelines which will help you to relax physically. Stand with arms over your head and try to reach up and touch the ceiling. Push hard, going up on tiptoe as far as you can. Then let your arms drop down to your side – limp. Repeat ten times. Next, sit in a chair and raise your right arm keeping every muscle tight. Make your arm as heavy as possible. Then let it drop – limp. Repeat this exercise five times. Then do the same exercise with your left arm. Next – with your knee bent raise your right leg, making it as heavy as possible. Then let it go – limp. Repeat this five times. Then do the same with your other leg. Then, as you sit in the chair, sit loose, every muscle relaxed. Picture yourself as a rag doll, no stiff muscles – you're limp. Remain like that for a minute or two. Finally, take several deep breaths – at least ten. Deep oxygen intake has a wonderfully calming effect on the body.

So much for physical relaxation. Let us now focus on mental relaxation. As the body becomes tied up with physical tensions so the mind becomes tied up with mental tensions. No amount of techniques of body relaxation will avail if there is tension in the mind. In Romans 12:2 we read "Do not conform any longer to the pattern of this world, but be transformed by the renewing of your mind". Note – when your mind is renewed you become a transformed person. The mind is the key. The mind, however, cannot be told to be calm and relaxed unless it rests in some assurance beyond itself. So learn to focus your mind on God. Draw from Him the strength and power you need. See yourself linked to Him through the sacrifice of His Son on Calvary. He is your God and you are His child. You are an heir of God and a joint heir with Christ. Assured of this position say to the organs of your inner being something like this: "My brain, you are now in the presence of God. Let go and listen. He speaks. He penetrates. He heals. Relax and receive." And to the nerves: "O nerves, the carrier of so many messages, strained and torn by living in a world of chaos, I now set you to work on the job of reporting better news – your God comes, comes with the good news of calm, of poise, of confidence, of redemption." And to every cell of your being, say, "I put you at God's disposal. He is now in every cell, bathing them with His gentleness, reinforcing every weakness, coordinating all parts and making them into a beautiful whole." Open every door of your being to Christ – give Him all the keys.

But deeper than the mind is the spirit. This is the central part of us: the motivating centre of our personality. How do we go about relaxing the spirit? We said earlier that techniques of relaxation are not enough in themselves. To really relax spiritually the spirit needs to have a firm grip upon God. "How did you like the aeroplane flight?" was asked of a nervous man who had just flown for the first time. "It was all right", he said, "but I never did put my full weight down." There can be no enjoyment of an aeroplane journey, or of this larger journey through life, unless we learn to put our whole weight down. Obviously there is nothing, absolutely nothing, upon which you can put your whole weight, except *God*. Those who refuse to do as the Quakers suggest and "settle down in God" but keep their troubles and disappointments in their own hands, are frustrated. There can never be complete spiritual relaxation unless that relaxation rests ultimately in the love and goodness of God. A relaxed spirit is one that knows and affirms this fact – God loves me and when at times He denies me the thing I ask, it is only because love and goodness in Him decided that I am not ready for it, it is not His will for me, or He will give me something better. The three Hebrew young men of Daniel's day said, "God ... is able to deliver us from the burning fiery furnace ... but if not ... we will not serve thy gods" (Daniel 3:17–18, AV). They did not rest their confidence in immediate deliverance but in the ultimate love and goodness of God. That is what produces a relaxed spirit. When at the depths of your being you hold and maintain the conviction that God always wills your good then you are ready to be engaged in the kind of praying that changes the world.

Nothing that happens can hurt me
Whether I lose or win
Though life may be changed on the surface
I do my main living within.

6

Begin your prayer time by **reading** a passage from **the Bible**

T ime spent with the Bible is usually the best preparation for prayer. A short meditation on some fragment of Scripture quickens the spirit of devotion and primes the heart in readiness for contact with God. George Muller, founder of the orphanages in Bristol, claimed that one of the greatest discoveries of his Christian experience was the way in which meditation on the Scriptures prepared him for deeper communion with the Lord.

Some Christians find a devotional aid such as *Every Day with Jesus*, or other types of devotional literature, to be a help in priming the pump of prayer. But they are secondary and not a substitute for a first-hand contact with the Word of God. Once you have read the Word of God you have done what a pilot does when he tunes up his engines preparatory to the commencement of a flight. The Word has started your thinking and your aspirations going in the right direction. It has aligned you with the will of God and where the will of God is done the power of God can come. In order to get the best out of your Scripture reading take these steps:

Come to the Word expectantly. The Bible is alive with hidden meaning: "For the Word of God is living and active" (Hebrews

4:12, RSV). Expect it to speak to you and it will. I am amazed at the number of Christians who open their Bibles, peruse its pages, but expect nothing to surprise them. They are seldom disappointed. Faith is expectancy – according to your expectancy be it unto you.

Come prepared to surrender to the truth it unfolds. One of the secrets of getting the best out of the Bible is contained in the word "obedience". To the extent that you are willing to obey, to that same extent will God's will be revealed. As you obey so He reveals. But when you stop obeying then the Book is shut. Although I have been a student of the Scriptures for over 50 years there are many times when I discover some truth in the Bible I have not seen before. I ask myself on these occasions: "Why haven't I seen that before?" The answer usually is that I have not, until this occasion, been ready to obey it. If there is in our heart a disinclination to obey, then revelation ceases to reveal.

Come expecting to use the truths God reveals to you. We must be ready not only to receive the truths revealed but to relay them through our personality to others. Nothing can really get into us unless it can get out of us. When God illuminates some truth or principle to our hearts, it is His intention that we not only use it for ourselves but that we pass it on to others.

Come leisurely and unhurriedly. If you go crashing through a forest you will probably see and hear very little. But sit quietly in the forest and soon the squirrels will come, the birds will begin to sing, the animals will draw near, and everything will come alive – because you are quiet and receptive. Little impression can be made on a tense, hurried, mind or spirit. But if you stop and wait, then the Word becomes alive with meaning.

Come believing it to be a divine revelation. The Bible, unlike any other book in the world, contains the *full* revelation of God for our lives. Approach it in this frame of mind and you will find it becomes self-authenticating to you. It will find you at your deepest depths.

You will know it is inspired, for you will find it inspiring. You will know that God is in it for God will come out of it. It is a revelation, for it reveals. It is an exhaustless mine. You may think, at times, that you have exhausted its riches, but then, as you wander along the shafts of meditation, you will discover new veins of gold – riches you never thought existed. Your whole being will become alert and receptive as you survey the wondrous store of God in His Word. One great writer said: "I expect my books to be exhausted of content within a few years – hence the new ones." But you can never exhaust the meaning of Jesus. Moffatt translates Luke 1:78 in this way: "Thanks to the tender mercies of our God who will cause the *dawn* to visit us from on high". Those who look for Jesus in His Word will find themselves living in a perpetual dawn. A surprise comes with every new day.

I know of some Christians who come to their morning quiet time without a Bible and just sit and think of anything that comes to mind. One couple told me, when I asked them if they had a daily quiet time, "Yes, we sit and smoke for a quiet half-hour after breakfast." They were sincere people, but living defeated Christian lives because they depended on the pitiable substitute of nicotine instead of the endless resources of God. I showed them how to go into a quiet time with God's Word, and when they learned to breathe God deep into the inner recesses of their being, they found they no longer needed nicotine, and relinquished the smoking habit.

If you begin your quiet time without a Bible and just sit enclosed with your own thoughts then you are likely to go off on a tangent, or become self-engrossed. Unless our thoughts are constantly corrected by God's thoughts then our thoughts go off in all directions, or mull around on themselves. So before attempting to get through to God in prayer start your quiet time by meditating on His Word. This means that you will get to God, not through the medium of your own conceptions, but through the medium of God's revelation of Himself. His thoughts become your thoughts. You are ready for anything.

7

Use a
notebook

This idea was given to me by an old Welsh miner many years ago, just after I was converted. "Keep a notebook when you go into your prayer time", he said, "it's easier to manage than prayer lists, and provides a more efficient record of your prayer vigils. On one side of the page write down all the things you want to bring before God, and on the other side the things God may say to you, or any specific answers to prayer you may have been given." At first I thought his idea much too mechanical to be of lasting spiritual benefit, but when I began to put it into practice I found it helped to deepen my relationship with God in a way that is impossible to describe.

We all know of occasions when something pops into our mind that we know we ought to bring before God in our personal prayer times. But unless we make a note of it there and then we may find that when we come to pray, the matter has slipped our minds. A prayer notebook would have captured that fleeting thought or idea and recorded it so that it would not have been forgotten. Similarly, when we hear of a prayer that has been answered, unless it is recorded there and then we may find ourselves forgetting the issue in our personal prayer time and thus make no special point of expressing our praise and gratitude to God for the answered prayer.

It goes without saying that a notebook, such as this, should be carried with you everywhere you go. Then whenever a matter of prayer concern comes to your attention, making a note of it there and then makes it a matter of permanent record. You might prefer to trust your memory but, in my experience, I have found the words of Confucius to be wise and powerful: "The faintest ink is better than the finest memory."

If you develop the art of listening to God which I described earlier there will be occasions in your prayer time when God will speak directly to you. Write it down. Later you may want to recollect what it was God said to you and if it is not written down the words of God may be lost in vague indefiniteness. Whilst planning this book I came across an old notebook which I used in college when preparing for the ministry. I was intrigued to see again the words God spoke to me when I was in a quandary about which church I should go to as pastor when I entered the ministry. There were two invitations. One in the north of England and one in Helston, Cornwall. The church in the north offered more security, had more people, and, to my mind, was much more appealing. But as I prayed about the matter the Spirit said, "Cornwall". That word was written down in my notebook and I vividly remember, some weeks later, being greatly tempted to change my mind. But when I consulted my notebook the issue was at once settled. The word was written there quite clearly – Cornwall. It helped reinforce the issue and saved me from hours of unnecessary struggle and prevarication.

I remember sharing this idea some years ago at a church where I was invited to speak on the subject of "Building an effective prayer life". During the discussion time, at the end of the talk, several people expressed the view that, whilst the idea of a notebook was fine for some Christians, those who were well organised for example, it might be extremely inhibiting for those who were inclined to be more extrovert and outgoing. One man said "I often get carried away in my prayer times and soar in the heavenlies with Christ. If I was to pull myself back to earth to consult a notebook I am afraid my prayer times would become extremely desultory and unappealing." I sympathised with his point of view because whilst aids and techniques are useful they must never become so binding that they restrict our personalities and thus reduce our effectiveness in prayer. Some time later I received a letter from the man concerned, saying that, although the idea I had presented about the notebook had not appealed to him, he became increasingly intrigued by the idea and had adopted it into his prayer life. This is what he wrote: "I rejected the point you made about the notebook, but I see now that I did so because deep down I was afraid of anything that demanded discipline in my life. God spoke to me about this and, as I began to discipline myself to record specific prayer requests, specific answers, and the things God said to me, I found that instead of losing the sense of spontaneity in prayer, which is part and parcel of my make-up, it has enabled me to have a more effective prayer life than ever before. The floods of prayer now have a channel to run down and I know the channel is growing deeper and deeper every day."

8

Develop a
prayer pattern

Decide firstly on how long your prayer time is going to be. Those who are experienced in prayer claim that they need at least half an hour to achieve effectiveness, but if this amount of time presents problems to you then begin with fifteen minutes. One can hardly get anywhere on less. Plan your time to cover the three following aspects. You will need to look at *God*. You will need to look at *yourself*. You will need to look at *others*. Divide your time into three sections so that you cover all these aspects. You can, of course, vary the timings on each aspect as God directs, but no sustained prayer pattern which omits these three areas will be in harmony with the best spiritual insights which have come out of the lives of great prayer warriors of the past.

Looking at God means adoring Him, praising Him and thanking Him for the multiplicity of His blessings toward you. Spend some time reflecting on the fact that you, a soiled sinner, are made welcome in the presence of a holy God, and that He encourages you not only to come but to *linger* in His presence. Let your mind run over the many reasons you have to be thankful. It's surprising how they mount up as you begin to list them one by one – home, friends, family, food, health, the church, and so on. If you do not enjoy some of the blessings I have listed, then think of the things you *do* enjoy. Ponder them until your heart overflows with gratitude and thanksgiving rises, because it must.

A man once told me that he had difficulty in following the first part of the prayer pattern I had presented to him, because he could "think of nothing to be thankful for". His problem was not so much that there wasn't anything to be grateful for, but that he failed to employ his mind in tracking down the blessings of God upon his life. Nothing to be grateful for! God forgive the thought. No appreciation of the mercy that chastens us in our pride and pleasure! Or the problems that drive us to distraction yet, at the same time, push us humbled, penitent and receptive into the arms of an omnipotent God. No regard for Christ, God's crucified Son, Saviour, Brother, Counsellor, Friend! For the Church of God. For the Love of God, encompassing, overshadowing, undergirding! We have only to *focus* our mind on recounting God's blessings, and endless causes for thanksgiving pass by in review.

Looking at yourself means praying about your own spiritual condition. Many teachers on the art of prayer might disagree with me here and say that prayer for oneself ought to be kept until last. The reason they give for so doing is to guard prayer from selfishness. "Keep your own needs to the last", they say, "this will guard your prayer time from self-centredness". There is some truth in what they say, of course, but experience has shown me that when people pray for their own spiritual condition first, the purification that begins in them spills over into the prayers they pray. When they are purified then their prayers are purified. So, at this stage of prayer, let one thought be predominant: How can I become more like Jesus? "Christ", someone said, "is a perfect mirror: He reflects a perfect likeness of the image which falls upon Him." Sometimes, friends and acquaintances will overlook our faults and exaggerate our good points, but Jesus will always give us an honest appraisal of ourselves. So as you look into the mirror of

Christ and measure your life alongside His, ask Him to show you any faults, imperfections or sins that need to be confessed and put right. The best place in all the world to see yourself is in Christ, because when you look at Him you not only see yourself as you really are, but He gives you the strength and the grace to do something about it. If there is something to be confessed to someone, an apology to be made, or a spiritual deficiency to be corrected, then make a note of it in your notebook. This means it will not be forgotten later.

Looking at others means praying for others. Keep lists of people you know who are in special need. Some Christians keep an urgent daily list and a weekly list as well. Mention people by name and tell God plainly what you would like Him to do for them – to heal their sickness, save their marriage, help them to find employment, and so on. This part of the prayer pattern is called *intercession*. It involves, of course, more than just praying for *people*. It can be extended to such things as special events, such as church activities, or needs in the community, nation, or the world. Dr W. E. Sangster, in his book *The Secret of Radiant Living,* presents the art of intercession in a way that, to me, is unequalled. He says, "First think of God: His greatness, Glory, Purity ... then think of the person for whom you are praying. Now draw the awareness of God (in His power and readiness to bless) and your awareness of the person you are praying for (in their need and inability) *together* in the crucible of your loving and believing heart. Hold them together as long as you can. A full minute or more. Fuse them in the flame of your affection. Small as your love is beside God's, it will stem like the solder of a joint."

Someone might raise the question at this stage: What about *petition*? When do I focus on praying for my own personal needs? Well, it can be done in the second section of the prayer pattern when looking at yourself, or you can, if you wish, leave your own personal requests right until the last moments or minutes of your prayer time. For my own part I have found that the more I have grown in my spiritual life, the less time I spend in asking God to meet my *personal* needs. In the early part of my Christian life petition took up almost all of my prayer time. Now it occupies only a minor part, sometimes just seconds. And why? Because I have an ever increasing conviction that the more I seek God for Himself and not for the things He can do for me, then He will see to it that I will get all the things I need. I think this is why Matthew 6:33 is fast becoming a favourite verse of mine: "But seek first his kingdom and his righteousness, and all these things will be given to you as well".

9

Offer up prayer in **Jesus' Name**

I t is a good thing, when preparing to pray, to give attention to the words of Jesus which state, "And I will do whatever you ask in my name, so that the Son may bring glory to the Father. You may ask me for anything in my name, and I will do it" (John 14:13–14). What does praying in Christ's Name really mean? It means more than just attaching the formula to the end of our prayers and saying, "This I ask in Jesus' Name" for, quite clearly, the formula could easily be attached to prayers that are crudely and utterly selfish. It means praying according to the *character* of Christ, or praying prayers that He would pray if He were in our shoes. God can only answer prayer if the prayer is in accord with the Spirit of Jesus Christ. Don't try to get God to do anything that is not Christlike. He just won't do it. In fact, He can't do it for it is impossible for God to do anything that is against His own nature.

Prayer is not trying to get God to do our will, but it is the bringing of our will into line with God's will. When we pray in the Name of Jesus we are asking that we might be so caught up in the Spirit of Christ, whose sole aim, you remember, was to do the will of His Father, that we will pray the kind of prayers that put

God's will as the highest priority in our lives, even though it may run counter to our own plans and desires.

There are some petitions we present to God of which if we were to stop and ask ourselves: "Can I be certain this is what He really wants?" we would have to say, in all honesty, "I don't know". At such times we can safely leave the outcome to God and say, "If it be thy will". Concerning many things, however, no shadow of doubt remains. We *know* God's will. We know that He desires the salvation of lost souls. We know that He wants to give us health of spirit, soul and body. We know that He wants to give us love, joy, peace, and so on. To wonder about these things is to wonder about something we ought never to wonder about at all. We *know*!

The more we soak ourselves in the principles of Scripture the more we will know what prayers we can offer in the Name of Jesus and for which we can rightfully press our claims. In the early days of my Christian experience, before I knew Scripture as I know it today, I found that my prayer life was filled with petitions for *things*. I prayed for money, for clothes, for a car, for books, and a whole host of other articles. Now, however, after 56 years as a Christian, I find an astonishing thing about my prayer life. I pray less and less for things and more and more to know God. I have an increasing conviction (as I said earlier) that the more I ask God for Himself, for the assurance that my will and His are not at cross-purposes, that we are in agreement on all major and minor matters, then I will get all the *things* I need.

Kagawa, the great Japanese Christian, when asked to give his definition of prayer, answered in one word – "Surrender". He was right. It is the surrender of our selfish desires in order that we might lock into God's desires – the giving up of self-interest in order to find an eternal interest. When I presented this concept of prayer to a counsellee, a businessman, he said to me: "But to surrender myself is just passive submission. I have to fight hard to keep my business on an even keel, and it is my ambition, with God's help, which has brought me where I am today. What you are suggesting seems to me a denial of the will to live." I replied that what I was saying was far removed from a denial of the will to live. Prayer is the will to die on the level of an empty, selfish, defeated, ineffective, short-circuited life, and the will to live on the level of a victorious, full, effective and abundant life. It is self-denunciation to find self-realisation. I told him of another businessman I knew who also couldn't come to terms with the idea of prayer as self-surrender and who had forged ahead in his business until the money he made choked his soul and brought him spiritual deterioration.

Prayer is the wire surrendering to the dynamo; the flower surrendering to the sun; the child surrendering to education; a branch surrendering to the vine. If we fear to surrender our wills to God in the event He might deprive us of something we feel is beneficial to us, or that we might lose our ambition, then we are greatly mistaken. A branch, if not surrendered to the vine, but cut off and on its own is not free, or fulfilled, but dead. A person who doesn't surrender to God isn't free; he is futile. He is like a blind man, with cataracts, who won't surrender his blindness to a surgeon in order to see. He is free – to remain blind.

Learn, therefore, to pray your prayers in the Spirit of Jesus Christ. Prayers that are undergirded by biblical principles. Prayers that put God first and self second. Prayers that Jesus would pray if He were in your shoes. To pray such prayers will not demean your personality but direct it – to God's ends. It is not a passive surrender but, as someone described it – "alert passivity". It is a passivity that awakens the whole being to the right kind of activity. The surrender is but a step to real mastery.

10

Listen for
God's voice

am astonished at the number of books that are written on the
subject of prayer that make no mention of cultivating the art of
active listening. Prayer is not just talking to God: it involves
listening as well. Prayer has been defined as "conversation with
God". All polite conversation is a two-way thing. It is the same with
prayer. We talk to God and He talks to us. After you have talked to
God then, before you rise from your knees, spend a minute or two
(more if possible) letting God talk to you.

But how does one cultivate the art of listening to God? And how
do we learn to recognise the voice of God when He speaks to us?
Some years ago I came across a passage in a book called *Creative
Prayer* by Mrs Herman (unfortunately now out of print) that for
me put the whole concept of listening to God in clear focus. I
quote the passage in full:

> The alert and courageous soul making its first venture upon
> the spiritual life is like a wireless operator on his trial trip in the
> Pacific. At the mercy of a myriad electrical whispers the novice
> at the receiver does not know what to think. How fascinating

they are, these ghostly pipings and mutterings, delicate scratchings and thick murmers – and how confusing! Now he catches the plaintive mutterings of a P & O liner trying to reach a French steamer, now the silvery tinkle from a Japanese gunboat seeking its shore station. There are aimless but curiously insistent noises, like grains of sand tumbling across tar paper: these are the so-called "static" noises of the atmosphere adjusting itself to a state of electrical balance.

Again, there comes a series of tuneless splashings – that is heat-lightning miles away – followed by the rumour of a thunderstorm in the opposite direction. Now he thinks he has got his message, but it is only the murmured greetings of ships that pass in the night. And then, just as his ear has begun to be adjusted to the weird babel of crossing sounds, there comes a remote and thrilling whisper that plucks at his taut nerves and makes him forget all his newly acquired knowledge. It is the singing of the spheres, the electrical turmoil of stars beyond the reach of the telescope, the birth cry and death wail of worlds. And when he is steeped soul-deep in the spell of this song of songs, there comes a squeaking, nervous spark, sharp as the squeal of a frightened rat. He decides to ignore it, and then suddenly realises that it is calling the name of his own boat. It is the expected message and he nearly missed it.

In the same way the Christian who waits and listens for the voice of God must learn to disentangle His voice from the other voices that clamour for his attention – the ghostly whisperings of the subconscious, the noise of traffic in the street, the sounds of children at play. To learn to keep one's ear true in so subtle a labyrinth of sound is indeed a venture. It doesn't come easy but the more we practise it the more we will be able to detect the voice of God when He speaks to us.

But what does God's voice *sound* like? An old lady in Wales told me many years ago that God is Welsh. I asked her why she thought that. She replied, "Well, He always speaks to me in that language!" Naturally God's voice will filter through our personalities and will come to us in the language or the idiom with which we are most familiar. But it is still God's voice for all that. God's voice is like the voice of conscience, only richer and more positive. Conscience merely approves or disapproves, but God's voice does much more. It informs, instructs, encourages and guides. It *never* argues but is quietly insistent and authoritative. Not every day will the voice of God be equally clear. The closeness of our walk with God will determine that and, of course, the divine awareness of our need. Jesus said in one passage in the New Testament that His sheep *know* His voice (John 10:4). They do. You may be saying at this moment, "I have been praying for years but I have never once heard the voice of God." Ah, but did you pray *believing* that God would speak to you? It is possible to pray, and pray often, without such a sense of expectation. Expect God to talk to you. Incline your ear unto Him and in time you will not be disappointed.

11

Open your whole being to the **flow of God's Spirit**

Sometimes one hears the expression: "I need all the help I can get." Ever said that? Well, if Christians are to exercise their rights and privileges at the place of prayer, achieve great victories and reach new spiritual heights, then they are going to need all the help they can get. We have all the help we need in the Person of the Holy Spirit.

Who is the Holy Spirit? He is the third Person of the Trinity and His executive function is to minister the resources of God and Christ to the weak and helpless believer. Listen to what Paul says on this subject in Romans 8:26: "In the same way, the Spirit helps us in our weakness. We do not know what we ought to pray for, but the Spirit himself intercedes for us with groans that words cannot express." The Holy Spirit helps us in many ways of course, but His chief aim and purpose is to enable us to pray, and pray effectively. John Wesley once said, "God does nothing in this world redemptively – except through prayer." Think of that for a moment. If it is true that God does nothing redemptively except through prayer then it means whenever God wants to do something important in a community, or even in a nation, He lays a prayerful burden deep in someone's heart and brings about change through the process of human/divine co-operation. God does nothing independently, but seeks to bring about change by working through His redeemed people in the place of prayer. Can you see therefore how prayer is vital to the running of the world?

But what if we don't feel greatly inclined to pray? Or we feel the burden is too great for us? Well, God gives us the help we need through the Person of the Holy Spirit. Take a look with me for a few moments at the Greek word for *help*. It is a combination of three words: *sun* – "along with"; *anti* – "on the opposite side"; and *lambano* – "to take hold of". When put together the word reads *sunantilambanotai*, which means "to join together and take hold of something on the other side". It might be worth mentioning in passing that Greek scholars point out this word is in the indicative mood and represents a fact. It is in the middle voice, indicating that the Holy Spirit is doing the action; it is in the present tense, that speaks of continuous action. In other words the Holy Spirit is always available to take hold on the other side of our prayer burdens and take the heavier end, so that with His co-operation and ours God can bring about change in the world.

The more you allow the Holy Spirit to flow into and through your life the greater will be your power in prayer. The great preacher of a past generation, C. H. Spurgeon, once declared, "We shall grow cold, unholy and worldly ... and Christ will be dishonoured unless we obtain a larger measure of the Holy Spirit." Samuel Chadwick, one time Principal of Cliff College, said, "Go back! Back to that Upper Room; back to your knees, back to searching of heart and habit, thought and life; back to pleading, praying, waiting till the Spirit of the Lord floods your soul with light and you are endued with the power from on high."

Andrew Murray, another great prayer warrior, emphasised the need for utter dependency on the Holy Spirit when he wrote: "In every prayer the triune God takes a part; the Father Who hears, the Son in Whose Name we pray, and the Holy Spirit Who prays for us and in us. How important it is that we should be in a right relationship to the Holy Spirit and understand His word!"

There are, of course, many doctrinal differences on the subject of the Holy Spirit. Some say we have the Spirit at our conversion and there is nothing more to seek. Others say we receive just one operation of the Spirit at conversion (regeneration) and we need to seek a further encounter with the Holy Spirit, which they describe as the baptism in the Spirit. At this moment I am not interested in arguing a doctrinal point, but want to encourage you to open your life to all that God has for you. If you believe that you received all of the Holy Spirit at conversion then what steps are you taking to ensure that His Spirit is flowing in your life to the extent He should? And if you believe that the Spirit came to you subsequent to your conversion and you were baptised with the Holy Spirit and fire, then how up to date is that experience? Is He flowing in you now with as much force and energy as He once did?

If we are to experience greater power in prayer then we must see to it that we take seriously Paul's admonition: "Be filled with the Spirit" (Ephesians 5:18). You will no doubt have heard someone say that the verse just quoted is in the present continuous tense in the Greek and should be read: "Be being filled with the Spirit". Whatever our experience in the past, let our eyes be uplifted, our hearts wide open for a greater supply of the Spirit to flow in us and through us than we have ever known before.

12

Cultivate
the power
of **imagination**

Some Christians speak disparagingly of the imagination. This is because they mistakenly classify it in their mind with fancy, fantasy, or speculation. But imagination is one of the greatest gifts God has given us. All great achievements, say our psychologists, belong first to the imagination. A newspaper article I once read, told the story of a young American who crossed the English Channel in a small aircraft which was kept aloft by nothing more than pedal power. As he pedalled this kept the propeller turning and in this way he made his journey, sometimes just a few feet above the waves, across the Channel. In an interview with a reporter he said, "I have flown this Channel a thousand times in my imagination. I have seen the water beneath my feet, seen the ships, the clouds, the occasional threat of a storm ... and then heard the cheers of the people as they saw me coming in to land." It was essential to his success that he flew the Channel in his imagination, or else (according to his own admission) he would never have flown it at all.

The proper use of the imagination is not to conjure up false or foolhardy things – that is fantasy – but to take things that are capable of achievement, albeit with great effort, and to turn them into reality. Many psychologists say that the imagination is ten times more powerful than the will. They say that if the will is set in one direction and the imagination is firmly set in another, the imagination will ultimately win. Part of the power of prayer is to harness the imagination and use it to turn ideas into facts.

How then do we employ imagination in prayer? Let's say that during your prayer time you become conscious of a number of spiritual deficiencies in your life. You become aware perhaps that you are lacking in genuine love, or joy – or even peace. Imagination comes to your aid when you *see yourself* receiving those qualities, and picture them flowing into you straight from the throne of God. Harness the imagination to your quest and you will discover that what the will cannot do, the imagination *used by the Holy Spirit* will bring into your life what you desire. Link imagination with affirmation and *say* it as well as see it. There is no doubt that God wants to give you His love, His joy, His peace, and indeed any other fruit of the Spirit of which you may be in need. You don't have to keep on asking for it, because through the blessings of imagination and affirmation it can flow right into you. Don't say, "Oh God, please, please, give me the love I need", but:

Lord, right now I am being filled with Your love.
Lord, right now I am being filled with Your peace.
Lord, right now I am being filled with Your joy.

Some Christians confuse the use of the imagination and affirmation with what is commonly called auto-suggestion. They are not the same thing. Auto-suggestion, as the name implies, is *self*-centred. Using the imagination in the way I have described centres on God. Auto-suggestion is used to trick the mind into believing what may not be true. The right use of the imagination deals only with truth. We have no right, of course, to use the imagination beyond its proper limits and to expect all our desires to come to pass. This is why before employing the imagination we must ask ourselves three questions: Is what I am asking for clearly the will of God? Am I sure beyond all doubt that God wants me to have this thing – and have it now? Is there any uncertainty in my mind about its truth?

There are those, of course, who find it difficult to *see* things in their imagination. They don't think in terms of pictures, and have difficulty in putting their imagination to work. Let them not despair. Practise a few moments every day developing an image of yourself in different situations. The proud you, becoming humble. The fearful you, holding your head up high. The resentful you, offering the hand of forgiveness. Just hold the picture there, if only for a few seconds. The discipline of the moments, if observed *daily*, will, I assure you, be infinitely rewarding. When imagination is used to picture the realised end of a situation and it is held clearly in the mind's eye, then all the doors of the personality fly open and the power of God floods in.

So see it done. Link imagination with affirmation and new power will flow into your prayers.

13

Outmanoeuvre
wandering thoughts

One of the biggest hindrances to an effective prayer life is the problem of mind wandering. Time and time again I have come across this problem when counselling Christians on the subject of effective praying. They say, "I know the value of prayer but I just can't beat this problem of mind wandering." This greatly distresses some people. How do we cope with this vexing problem? When the mind wanders, let the thing to which it wanders become the focus of your praying. When I was writing this chapter I looked out of the window and my attention was suddenly caught by *Concorde* flying past (I lived near London Airport at the time). For a few minutes my thoughts began to wander and then, remembering my own advice, I began to focus on the crew and passengers of the plane. I asked God to keep them safe and to give everyone on board an understanding of His love for them as expressed in the Cross. My mind wandered, but in the end it wandered to God.

A lady once said to me in a counselling session: "But I am distracted by *anything*. The slightest noise in the house, the sound of barking dogs, an ambulance or police siren in the distance ..."

At the moment she was speaking a police car went by with its siren sounding and I said, "Now let's put my advice to the test. Now that your mind is focused on the siren how will you use it to aid rather than defeat your prayer life?" She thought for a moment and bowed her head in the counselling room and prayed this prayer. "O Lord, this siren is distracting me but I realise it is just a warning for people to move out of the way so that the police, or ambulance, might get to the emergency faster. Father, I am so deadened to the plight of those who are lost and going to hell that I, too, need to be alerted by an even louder siren than this. Make me aware of the danger by which men and women are threatened without Christ." Tears ran down her face as she prayed that prayer. The distraction has become a direction – to God.

If you are beset by wandering thoughts, perhaps even *evil* thoughts then, instead of wrestling with them, trying to beat them down, use them as a prayer focus. A man I know was afflicted by evil thoughts the moment he got down to prayer. Lustful images would rise unbidden into his mind. Unable to cope with the problem he gave up on his prayer life and soon he came for counselling – defeated and downcast. He was shown how to take each lustful thought and use it to God's ends. This is how it was done.

When a lustful thought entered his mind (in his case, a naked woman or an erotic bedroom scene) he was advised not to try and push it from his mind (that merely uses up emotional energy to no good purpose) but to picture Christ standing with him, looking on the image in his mind. He would then, in his imagination, turn to Christ and pray along this line: "Lord, you can see this image that is before me. I know it comes from that part of my nature that is carnally inclined. Sex was designed by You to be beautiful and clean, but in my thoughts it has become defiled and impure. Fill my imagination with such a picture of You that it will take up the whole perspective of my thoughts." As this man learned to focus his imagination on Jesus and use these moments to develop a conversation with Christ, he found, after a while, that whereas before he was unable to dismiss the thoughts with a peremptory word, they were now elbowed out by the vision of Jesus that he held in his mind. Christ is the centre of all things pure. Lustful images steadily dissolve on the steady gaze of His searching eyes. The thing that looked so seductive a moment before looks loathsome with Jesus consciously present. Coolness in the place of heat, and serenity instead of desire, are the reward of those who are swift to bring Jesus alongside the pictures that enter the mind. The man told me some months later that practising this method of overcoming mind wandering made Jesus more real to his heart than He had ever been before. "I have such a clear picture of Christ in my mind and I have developed the art of conversational prayer to such a great degree," he said, "that, although I hesitate to say it, I feel almost thankful that I was plagued with these evil thoughts, as they have become the stepping stones to a more personal and dependent relationship with the Lord."

Any Christian, bent on winning the battle over evil thoughts, can, by using the method I have described above, outmanoeuvre the problem in a few weeks, or at the most a few months. Distracting thoughts can be handled in the way I have shown in a matter of days. It takes a little time to get into the habit of dealing with issues in the manner described, but after a while, and with practice, you will be able to bring every thought into captivity to the obedience of Christ.

14

Add power by entering into an **occasional fast**

The New Testament makes clear that some spiritual victories can only be experienced when we know how to *fast* as well as pray. On one occasion Jesus said to His disciples, who were having some difficulty in casting out a demon from a possessed boy, "But this kind of demon won't leave unless you have prayed and gone without food" (Matthew 17:21, Living Bible). Fasting is the practice of deliberately abstaining from food in order to add greater power to one's prayers.

No study of prayer could ever be complete without a careful look at the importance of fasting in relationship to prayer. Let's bring a few facts into focus concerning this important spiritual exercise.

(a) Fasting puts the body in its place. God has designed us with three powerful drives – the spiritual (spirit), the psychological (soul) and the physical (body). Effective Christian living flows from a right relationship of these three drives. If the spiritual part of our being is strongest then it will keep the psychological and physical drives in their proper place. In the Old Testament

(Leviticus 16:29) God instructed the children of Israel to set aside a special day annually for the purpose of "afflicting their souls" (AV). It was called the Day of Atonement. The word "afflict" seems to suggest that the fasting that was required on the Day of Atonement was the means by which man's spirit took authority over his body. This was achieved by abstaining from food. Abstinence causes pain to the body because it has become accustomed to the regular intake of food. Paul, in the New Testament, takes up a similar point when he says, "No, I beat my body and make it my slave so that after I have preached to others, I myself will not be disqualified for the prize" (1 Corinthians 9:27). When a Christian practises the art of fasting his spirit says to his body: "You will not dictate the terms of my life; I'm the boss – and don't forget it." We can only conquer the enemy (Satan) after we have conquered ourselves.

(b) Fasting gives victory over temptation. There can be no doubt that Christ's victory over Satan in the wilderness (Matthew 4:1) was due, in no small measure, to His forty days' fast. No one is exempt from temptation. Because of this we need all the available power we can get to resist and withstand Satan's wiles. Fasting reinforces the human spirit, enabling it to deal more efficiently and effectively with the devil's strategies. Professor Hallesby, writing on the theme of fasting in relation to victory over temptation, says, "To make use of a rather mechanical, but nevertheless vivid, illustration, we might compare fasting with the transmission of electrical power. The greater the volume of power to be transmitted the stronger must be the connection with the power house. Fasting helps to give us that inner sense of spiritual penetration by means of which we can discern clearly that for which the Spirit of prayer would have us pray in exceptionally difficult circumstances."

(c) Fasting sharpens our spiritual understanding enabling us to make right decisions. Is it not significant that Jesus spent a night in prayer before choosing His disciples? I have found in my own life that to precede the making of an important decision with a 24-hour fast enables me to come to the moment of decision with clarity and conviction. Speaking in purely biological terms a Christian doctor says: "When we eat, then a good deal of blood is directed to the stomach by the brain to aid the processes of digestion. When we abstain from food there is a great blood flow to the brain enabling it to function at its very best." Whatever way we look at it, physically or spiritually, fasting helps to clear the mind of the distractions that might hinder the making of wise decisions.

Church history shows that many of the men who figured greatly in the growth and development of the Christian Church practised the art of fasting. John Wesley so believed in the importance of fasting that he refused to ordain young men to the ministry who would not fast two days each week. Martin Luther fasted regularly, and so did John Knox. Charles Finney said, "When empty of power I would set apart a day for private fasting and prayer ... after this, the power would return in all its freshness."

I am convinced myself that if Christians were to fast as well as pray we would see a move of the Holy Spirit throughout the world, such as we have not seen since the days of the Early Church. If you have never fasted before and you want to learn the art, then begin in a small way by entering into a 12- or 24-hour fast. Believe me, fasting is not easy. The first time I tried to fast I could go no longer than six hours! But I persisted and within a year I was able to fast for a week without any difficulty at all. No one should enter on a long fast before checking with a doctor. And if you have serious medical problems (such as diabetes) then fasting is not for you.

15

Understand and **practise** the principles of faith

One great writer on the subject of prayer, said: "A person's prayer life is only as strong as that person's faith in God." Because faith is essential to effective praying we must put this important word under the spiritual microscope and examine it in detail. Faith is simply trust – it is confidence in the ability of God to do what He promises to do in His Word. Corrie Ten Boom labels faith as a "fantastic adventure in trusting Him". The dictionary defines faith as "trust in the honesty and truth of another". If we are to be effective in prayer then we must believe God is honest in what He says in the Bible.

The Bible contains many references to faith. There is saving faith spoken of by Paul in Ephesians 2:8. There is the "gift of faith" again spoken by Paul in 1 Corinthians 12:9. The great Apostle also speaks in Ephesians of the "unity in the faith" (Ephesians 4:13). The faith of which I am now speaking, however, is what some describe as *simple* faith – the innate ability to *trust*. John Bisagno, speaking of simple faith, says, "Don't get the idea that if you can only muster more faith, you will be effective in prayer. Faith is not some mysterious commodity to be sought after. You do not need more faith: you need to learn to appropriate the faith you already have ..." It is important to see, of course, that John Bisagno is focusing here on the innate ability we all have, to trust and believe. He is not speaking of the "gift of faith" nor of any other kind of faith, and his words must not be pressed out of context. Every man and woman on the face of the earth has a basic ability to believe and trust, and when they exercise that ability they are exercising faith. A theologian in the 18th century said that faith consisted of three parts; knowledge, self-committal and trust. Dr Billy Graham, taking up this definition, says; "I know from what I read that a jet plane can take me from New York to London. That is knowledge – the first ingredient of faith. But unless I take the next step – *self-committal* – and step on board the aircraft then I have no hope of getting to my destination. But even then faith is not complete, for unless I *trust* myself to the aircraft, and completely surrender to its efficiency, I will sit in my seat with great apprehension, fear and insecurity."

Faith, in terms of our present thinking in relation to prayer, can be described as follows: it is the willingness to act on God's Word with complete abandonment and total trust. The Apostle Peter provides a good example of this – he was willing to act on one single word of Jesus, "Come". When he acted on that word he was able to walk on water (Matthew 14:29). When we believe, *really* believe, we act as if we have what God has promised, irrespective of whether we can actually see the answer to our prayers or not. John Bisagno shares a touching story on this point. His five-year-old daughter came to him one day, whilst he was in his study, and asked him to build her a doll's house. He promised that he would and then went back to reading his book. "Soon", he says, "I glanced out of the window and saw my daughter with her arms filled with dishes, toys and dolls, making her pilgrimage to the corner of the yard where, by now, she had gathered a pile of playthings. I asked my wife what the purpose of this impossible pile could be." "You promised her a doll's house", she replied, "and now she believes in you. She's just getting ready for it." John said, "I threw the book aside, raced to the lumber yard for supplies, and quickly built my little girl the doll's house."

God delights in faith. The Scripture says, "... anyone who comes to him must believe that he exists and that he rewards those who earnestly seek him" (Hebrews 11:6). The greatest thing we can do to please God is believe Him! I have suggested earlier that it is important to read the Word of God before we pray, but another reason for this is because the reading of God's Word quickens our faith. "Faith cometh by hearing", says Paul, "and hearing by the word of God" (Romans 10:17, AV). God's Word produces faith, and faith produces power for prayer. Prayer, faith and the Word of God are directly related. They strengthen one another.

So when you pray, begin to exercise the muscles of your faith by committing yourself more and more to what God has promised you in His Word. Step out in faith, as Peter did on the water. You may feel yourself sinking at times, but don't worry – the Lord will be on hand to deliver you. The more you exercise your faith the more expert you will become in the art of prayer. You see it is not enough to simply ask God for things, we must *believe* for them also. Jesus said, "Therefore I tell you, whatever you ask for in prayer, believe that you have received it, and it will be yours" (Mark 11:24). Remember again our definition of faith – *the willingness to act on God's Word with complete abandon and trust*. If you are sure that what you ask is according to God's Word then don't just ask for it, *believe* for it. The initiative is in heaven. Only your unbelief can stop it coming out.

NATIONAL DISTRIBUTORS

UK (and countries not listed below):
CWR, PO Box 230, Farnham, Surrey GU9 8XG.
Tel: 01252 784710 Outside UK (44) 1252 784710

AUSTRALIA: CMC Australasia, PO Box 519, Belmont, Victoria 3216.
Tel: (03) 5241 3288

CANADA: CMC Distribution Ltd., PO Box 7000, Niagara on the
Lake, Ontario LOS 1JO.
Tel: 1 800 325 1297

GHANA: Challenge Enterprises of Ghana, PO Box 5723, Accra.
Tel: (21) 222437/223249   Fax: 226227

INDIA: Crystal Communications, Plot No. 83, Sesachalla Society,
Entrenchment Road, East Marredpalli, Secunderabad, Andhra
Pradesh 500 026.
Tel: (40) 7732511/7730577

KENYA: Keswick Bookshop, PO Box 10242, Nairobi.
Tel: (02) 331692/226047

MALAYSIA: Salvation Book Centre (M) Sdn. Bhd., 23 Jalan SS 2/64,
47300 Petaling Jaya, Selangor.
Tel: (603) 78766411/78766797 Fax: (603) 78757066

NEW ZEALAND: CMC New Zealand Ltd., Private Bag, 17910 Green
Lane, Auckland.
Tel: 09 5249393 Fax: 09 5222137

NIGERIA: FBFM, (Every Day with Jesus), Prince's Court, 37 Ahmed
Onibudo Street, PO Box 70952, Victoria Island.
Tel: 01 2617721, 616832, 4700218, 2619156

PHILIPPINES: Praise Incorporated, 145 Panay Avenue, Cor Sgt
Esguerra St, Quezon City.
Tel: 632 920 5291   Fax: 920 5747

REPUBLIC OF IRELAND: Scripture Union, 40 Talbot Street,
Dublin 1.
Tel: (01) 8363764

SINGAPORE: Campus Crusade Asia Ltd., 315 Outram Road, 06–08
Tan Boon Liat Building, Singapore 169074.
Tel: (65) 222 3640

SOUTH AFRICA: Struik Christian Books (Pty Ltd), PO Box 193,
Maitland 7405, Cape Town.
Tel: (021) 551 5900

SRI LANKA: Christombu Books, 27 Hospital Street, Colombo 1.
Tel: (1) 433142/328909

TANZANIA: City Christian Bookshop, PO Box 33463, Dar es
Salaam.
Tel: (51) 28915

UGANDA: New Day Bookshop, PO Box 2021, Kampala.
Tel: (41) 255377

USA: CMC Distribution, PO Box 644, Lewiston, New York
14092–0644.
Tel: 1 800 325 1297

ZIMBABWE: Word of Life Books, Shop 4, Memorial Bldg.,
35 S Machel Ave., Harare.
Tel: 781305   Fax: 774739

For e-mail addresses, visit the CWR web site: www.cwr.org.uk

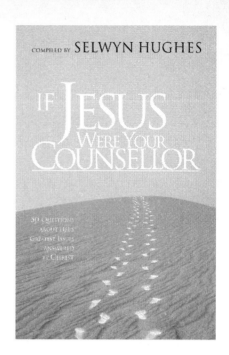

COMPILED BY **SELWYN HUGHES**

IF JESUS
WERE YOUR
COUNSELLOR

50 QUESTIONS
ABOUT LIFE'S
GREATEST ISSUES
ANSWERED
BY CHRIST

■ If Jesus were
your Counsellor

If Jesus were your Counsellor
offers 50 biblical answers from
the lips of Jesus to questions
about faith and life. Selwyn
Hughes brings more than four
decades of counselling
experience to this easy-to-follow
and beautifully designed book
which finds all its answers in
The Message translation of God's
Word. As well as being great for
personal use, this book is an
excellent aid to anybody
involved in "people helping".

ISBN 1-85345-152-5

■ £6.95

Available from Christian bookshops or by post from National Distributors

■ Signature Series

Born to Praise and *Discovering Life's Greatest Purpose* are based on the *Every Day with Jesus* devotionals. Each lavishly designed book contains undated lessons that take just a few minutes to read each day. Daily scriptures are supported by a commentary from Selwyn Hughes, a prayer, and space for personal journal entries.

■ £6.95 each

■ In *Born to Praise* Selwyn Hughes reveals the essential tools for a life of effective worship.

ISBN 0–80542–091–6

■ *Discovering Life's Greatest Purpose* teaches us how to be sensitive to the needs of others.

ISBN 0–80542–323–0

■ *Prayer – The Greatest Power* leads us towards a deeper experience of prayer that could revolutionise our lives.

■ In *God – The Enough* Selwyn challenges us to always depend on the grace and sufficiency of God.

Available from Christian bookshops or by post from National Distributors

Selwyn Hughes

5

Insights to
Discovering Your
Place in the
Body of
Christ

The Discipleship Series

Selwyn Hughes

10

Principles
for a Happy
Marriage

The Discipleship Series

■ The Discipleship Series

The *Discipleship Series* combines
practical advice with biblical principles
to bring you an invaluable collection of
books. Each title considers some of the
most vital aspects of Christian living,
such as marriage, prayer, discipleship
and the Church. Essential reading!

■ *5 Insights to Discovering Your Place
in the Body of Christ*

ISBN 1–85345–175–4

■ *10 Principles for a Happy Marriage*

ISBN 1–85345–173–8

■ £3.99 each

Available from Christian bookshops or by post from National Distributors

World-renowned

Christian Training and Resources

Ministry to Women

Counselling Training

Day and Residential Courses

Biblical Studies Courses

Regional Seminars

Books and Devotionals

Seminar Videos

Audio Cassettes

Located near Farnham in Surrey, in beautiful Waverley Abbey House, CWR have been involved in training and publishing for 35 years. Our daily devotional, *Every Day with Jesus*, is read by nearly half-a-million people around the world, and our courses in biblical studies and pastoral care and counselling are renowned for their excellence and spiritual impact. To find out more, phone the number below, write to us, or visit our web site – http://www.cwr.org.uk.

For your free brochure about our seminars and courses or a catalogue of CWR products, please phone 01252 784731 or write to:
CWR, Waverley Abbey House, Waverley Lane, Farnham, Surrey GU9 8EP.

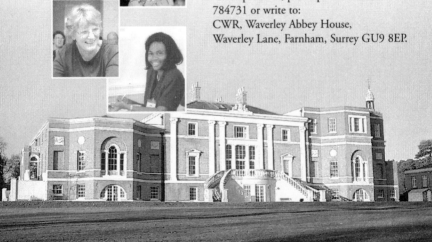